Pubs of Merton
(Past & Present)

by

Clive Whichelow

Published by

Enigma Publishing
4 Charnwood Avenue
London SW19 3EJ

First edition September 2003

ISBN 0 9524297 3 X

By the same author:

Mysterious Wimbledon (with Ruth Murphy)
More Mysterious Wimbledon (with Ruth Murphy)
Pubs of Wimbledon Village
Secrets of Wimbledon Common & Putney Heath
The Local Mystery of Robin Hood
Local Highwaymen

Printed by Wellington Press

CONTENTS

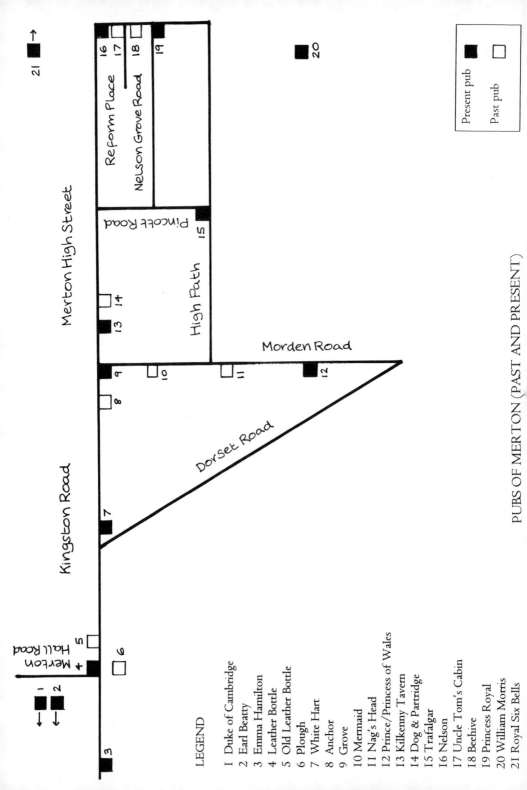

PUBS OF MERTON (PAST AND PRESENT)

LEGEND

1 Duke of Cambridge
2 Earl Beatty
3 Emma Hamilton
4 Leather Bottle
5 Old Leather Bottle
6 Plough
7 White Hart
8 Anchor
9 Grove
10 Mermaid
11 Nag's Head
12 Prince/Princess of Wales
13 Kilkenny Tavern
14 Dog & Partridge
15 Trafalgar
16 Nelson
17 Uncle Tom's Cabin
18 Beehive
19 Princess Royal
20 William Morris
21 Royal Six Bells

Present pub ■
Past pub □

INTRODUCTION

Whoe'er has travelled life's dull round
Where'er his stages may have been
May sigh to think he still has found
The warmest welcome at an inn
William Shenstone 1714-1763

The first thing to do when discussing Merton's pubs is to define which ones are actually in Merton. The Parish of Merton has ancient, and not always logical, boundaries.

So in Kingston Road for example, we find that the Leather Bottle, on the north side of the road, is in Merton, while the Duke of Edinburgh, also on the north side (which stood on the site now occupied by the fire station) was in Wimbledon. The King's Head, although in Merton High Street, is also in Wimbledon, while the Royal Six Bells, a few hundred yards away, is in Mitcham! And how many people will have realised that the Duke of Cambridge, lurking under the flyover at Shannon Corner, is in fact in Merton?

The good news is that Merton does have plenty of pubs, past and present, many with interesting stories to tell, and two dating back over three centuries.

In days gone by, inns and taverns were important social centres as well as being venues for village events and meetings. Manor courts and inquests were held at the White Hart in Kingston Road and it was the venue for the sale of Lord Nelson's estate in 1823. It was also the site of the village fair.

It is not an exaggeration to say that before the 20th century the public house was the main social centre of a community. Even during the 20th century, clubs that had an independent existence often held meetings, dinners, galas, rallies, and other social events at the pub, whether these groups were angling clubs, operatic societies or freemasons' gatherings. The only other focal point for most villages was the church, and even their vestry meetings were often held at the local inn.

Tracing the history of Merton's pubs gives some insight into the changes in society over the last three hundred years. Although today the pub is just one of the many places of meeting or entertainment it retains a special place in national life which may not be superseded.

ANCHOR

Two inches to the north-west is written a word full of meaning
- the most purposeful word that can be written on a map. 'Inn'
A.A. Milne 1882-1956

The Anchor in Kingston Road is one of Merton's lost pubs and was only in existence for around ten years.

In the 1871 census the proprietor, Robert Sparke, was described as a 'plumber and beer retailer', so the Anchor was unlikely to have been a substantial business, just a small beer house providing additional income for a local tradesman.

The exact position of the pub is not known, but it was, according to local writer W. H. Chamberlain, at the beginning of the south-western side of Kingston Road, just a few doors down from the Grove Hotel, by a row of small cottages.

Perhaps it was its proximity to the Grove that prevented this beer house from lasting longer than it did, although the Grove was probably catering for a rather more well-heeled clientele than the Anchor.

The last mention of Robert Sparke is in the directory of 1881 and he appears to have been the sole proprietor of the Anchor, again suggesting that it was a rather small beer house with no ambitions to be anything grander.

THE BEER ACT

The Anchor is a good example of the mass of small beer houses that sprang up in the wake of the 1830 Beer Act. This act, introduced by the Duke of Wellington, was designed to entice people away from the evils of gin-drinking by providing more beer houses that could not sell spirits. Prior to this, licences for taverns and inns were more difficult to obtain and then suddenly anyone who could pay two guineas for a licence was in business as a beer retailer. Most of Merton's pubs began after this act.

BEEHIVE

This beer house may well have been the forerunner to a later public house but the only mention of it anywhere as the Beehive is in the census of 1861, and the exact location is not given. It was in the Abbey Road/Nelson Grove Road area.

The beer retailer, Alexander Roots, is listed in the 1860 directory too, but nowhere else. A few years later, the Corner Pin was established in a similar location at the junction of Reform Place and Abbey Road (see separate entry), but at that time beer houses were springing up and disappearing quickly so it is difficult to be certain if it was the same pub. The Princess Royal, actually at the junction of Nelson Grove Road and Abbey Road, had already been established by 1860, so the Beehive was definitely a separate pub from this.

BRICKLAYERS' ARMS

This pub, in Merton High Street has had more name changes than any other in Merton. It has variously been known as the Horse & Groom, the Dark House, and today, the Kilkenny Tavern. It was also listed in the 1871 census as the Builder's Arms, though this may simply have been an error.

The first mention of the name Bricklayers' Arms appears in Trim's directory of 1881, but the first proprietor of the business was one Charles Deacon who was there from 1860 to 1876. By 1878 he had been succeeded by Mary Ann Deacon, presumably his widow, and in 1880 by Joseph Deacon, probably a son. Joseph was still there the following year when the pub acquired its name.

CORNER PIN

When this little corner beer house opened in Abbey Road in 1868 there were already two other pubs within a hundred yards in either direction: the Princess Royal at the corner of Nelson Grove Road, and the Nelson Arms near the junction with Merton High Street. This beer house, at the corner of Reform Place, was the predecessor to Uncle Tom's Cabin (see separate entry). The name Corner Pin doesn't appear in local directories until 1881, but the first proprietor, James Penfold, had started the beer house in 1868 and remained there until 1890. In that year petty sessions records show that it was being run by Hannah Penfold, his widow, and that it was owned by the Phoenix Brewery.

It seems extraordinary now that three separate pubs (Nelson Arms, Princess Royal, and this one) could happily flourish within a one hundred-yard stretch of a small side road. But the Nelson was probably aiming at a more middle-class clientele, and had the advantage of a full licence, and such was the demand for working-class beer houses, perhaps in the absence of any other form of cheap entertainment, that they happily co-existed for many years.

DARK HOUSE 1990

DARK HOUSE

This pub, as mentioned, was originally the Bricklayers' Arms, and later, the Horse and Groom. It was officially renamed the Dark House, its nickname, in 1984, and then reverted briefly to the Horse and Groom between 1995 and 1996 before the name changed again, to the Kilkenny Tavern in 1997 (see separate entries for other names, and also the Pub Names section).

The possible reasons for the name the Dark House are mentioned in the Pub Names section, but it may be significant that the two licensees prior to the present one both died at the pub, one after falling down the stairs.

MERTON AS A VILLAGE

When Lord Nelson came to live in Merton in 1801 it was a village of little more than 800 people. It is said that the rural charm was part of the attraction for him. At this time Merton only had two inns, the White Hart and the Leather Bottle, which had both been here for over a century. Fifty years later, there were five pubs in Merton serving a population of more than 2000. Another fifty years on, in 1901, the population was over 4500 and there were fifteen pubs. Despite this growth older residents can remember the farms and fields and the stiles and streams that were still here as late as the 1920s. The growth in population continued of course, and the extension of the underground to South Wimbledon (although so named, the station is in Merton) brought more expansion to the area. Surprisingly, there were no more pubs built in Merton after the Dog & Partridge in 1878 until the Earl Beatty opened in 1938.

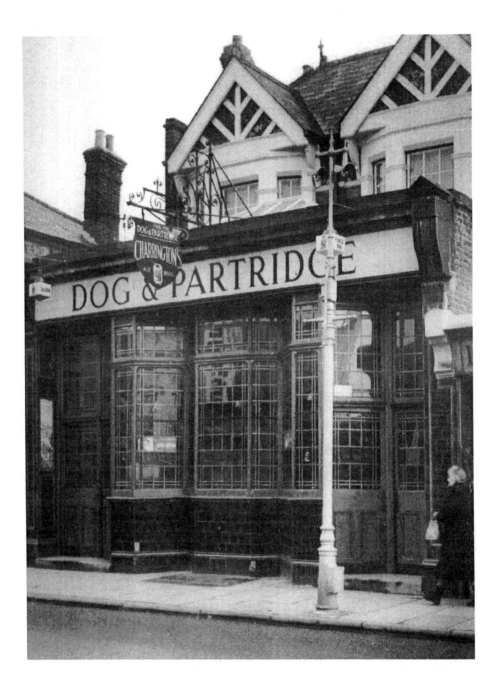

DOG & PARTRIDGE 1953

DOG & PARTRIDGE

What two ideas are more inseparable
than beer and Britannia?
Rev. Sydney Smith 1771-1845

The earliest mention of the name is in Trim's 1881 directory, but the proprietor, William Pincham, had been there since 1878. The pub, which stood at 101 Merton High Street, was there until 1974, but was pulled down as part of the High Path estate redevelopment. It was not owned by a brewery to begin with, and records show that in 1890 it was owned by one Mrs Morrison, and was being run by Elizabeth Pincham, widow of William.

Writing in 1925, W.H. Chamberlain remembers the popular landlord, Jimmy Evans, and the large taproom which was used as a club by locals for games of cards and dominoes. He recalls that on the wall was a picture of a sea battle, painted by an old sailor in honour of Lord Nelson. The beer and porter were brought round in large cans by the potman, and at Christmas every customer was given a large plate of boiled beef and carrots, with any leftovers going to the poor.

But by 1974 the redevelopment of the area threatened the pub with closure and the Wimbledon News of October 4th reported that regulars were organising a petition to save it. Some had been using the pub for forty years and the landlord said he had a photograph of the pub dated 1905 when it was being run by a master butcher, and that it had not changed very much in that time. Reference was also made to the 'enormous' stained-glass windows at the front of the pub.

Despite the protestations and petition the redevelopment went ahead and the Dog & Partridge was sadly demolished.

"DUKE OF CAMBRIDGE" SHANNON CORNER
KINGSTON BY PASS ROAD

DUKE OF CAMBRIDGE c.1930

DUKE OF CAMBRIDGE

It may surprise some people to find that the Duke of Cambridge is in Merton at all, being situated as it is at Shannon Corner. However, it is within the parish of Merton as the western boundary is formed by the Beverley Brook.

The pub opened in 1925, a year after construction work had begun on the new Kingston by-pass. The road was completed in 1927, the first major by-pass in the country, and the pub no doubt benefited from the increased passing trade.

At that time the pub had only a beer licence, and applied for a full licence in 1934, and despite some objection to this it was obtained. The objectors, including local residents, pointed out that when the pub was built a full licence was not wanted, and not envisaged for the future. This was countered by the licensee's point that the by-pass had significantly increased demand. This of course was before modern drink-driving laws and sensibilities.

The by-pass had a significant impact on the area. When the Duke of Cambridge first opened it was a semi-rural area, but by 1931 the farms had disappeared to be replaced by streets, shops, houses, and an additional 6000 people. Hundreds more houses were built in the next few years, and what was lost to semi-rural life was a substantial potential clientele for the Duke.

When the flyover was built in the mid-1960s the pub had to be altered to accommodate it. Beforehand there were five windows and a central door facing the A3 road, but the door and one of the windows were removed when the pub was partially rebuilt to allow for the flyover. This new development cannot have been of much advantage to the pub's trade, but at least the entire building did not have to be demolished for the sake of the flyover.

Today the pub is owned by Six Continents Brewery, formerly Bass.

THE SUICIDE ROAD

From the outset, concerns were expressed about the potential dangers posed by the new Kingston by-pass. When Prime Minister Stanley Baldwin opened it on October 28th 1927, he asked if there would be adequate facilities available to cope with casualties. In the 1960s, following the many accidents envisaged by Baldwin that had actually taken place, the Sunday Times dubbed the by-pass The Suicide Road in a special article.

EARL BEATTY 2003

EARL BEATTY

This is another pub which many will be surprised to find is in Merton. Situated in West Barnes Lane near Motspur Park station, it was built in 1938 and the first landlord was Mr E.R. Stradwick.

Because of its being named after the Admiral of the Fleet the pub has long had a décor with a naval theme. Before a refurbishment in 1973 it had large murals of battleships as well as portraits of Earl Beatty and the ubiquitous Lord Nelson. These latter two were retained in the refurbishment but the murals went, to be replaced by ratlines, rigging and storm lights.

Some of the locals were not impressed with the change or the fact that the pub became open-plan too. But it remained popular with local cricket teams who played at the nearby Joseph Hood Memorial playing fields and popped in for a pint or two between innings!

Today the pub is owned by Scottish and Newcastle and is still popular with sportsmen and women. Local football, hockey and cricket teams regularly use the pub as do a professional football club – Fulham FC - who train next door.

Current visitors may be surprised to find that, despite the naval connections of the pub, there is one bar full of model aeroplanes! Known to regulars as the War Room, this bar's collection of planes began after the first Gulf War in 1991, when some of the regulars were discussing aircraft. The discussion prompted one regular to bring in a model, and this was followed by more and more, leading to the impressive collection that can be seen today. What Earl Beatty would have made of it we can only guess.

EMMA HAMILTON 2002

EMMA HAMILTON

Beer, happy produce of our isle
Can sinewy strength impart
And wearied with fatigue and toil
Can cheer each manly heart
Caption to Hogarth's Beer Street

This is one of the newest of Merton's pubs, which celebrated its fortieth anniversary in December 2002, although the idea of a pub on this site had first been mooted as far back as 1936. The opening of the pub at this time was opposed not only by the Merton Park Baptist church who would have been a near neighbour, but also by the owners of Ye Olde Leather Bottel just along Kingston Road who feared losing trade to this new rival.

The pub was to be named the Earl Jellicoe, and despite a 1000-name petition in support of the application it was turned down.

All was quiet again until February 1961 when, with the closure of the Plasterers' Arms in South Road, Wimbledon, a licence was available. Despite protestations from the Wimbledon, Merton and Morden Church Council, the Earl Jellicoe, which was still to be the name of the pub, was to open in 1962.

Unusually, the brewery, Watney Combe Reid, decided to poll the public on the choice of name for the new pub. Out of the 1232 people polled seventy-five suggested the Lady Hamilton and each was awarded two dozen cans of Watney's Pale Ale. Of course the final name was the rather more familiar Emma Hamilton, but this ensured its uniqueness as there is a pub named the Lady Hamilton at Neston in Cheshire.

Apart from the addition of a restaurant to the pub in 1973 it has changed little though it is owned today by the Top Dog Pub Company.

MERTON. — THE GROVE HOTEL.

GROVE TAVERN c.1910

GROVE TAVERN

Unusually, a precise date is available for the opening of this pub: May 26th 1865, when it was being run by Richard Hall. Despite the rather grand name of the Grove Hotel the original pub was described in its lease as a 'beer house'. However, by 1890 it had a spirit licence and was being run by Henry Cockle.

In 1895 the freehold of the pub was sold to Cannon Brewery for £2850. In 1924 numbers 1-4 The Parade (shops) and the freehold were sold by a Mrs Eagles to the City of London and Suburban Railway Company and nine years later they sold them to Cannon Brewery. The pub was later owned by Taylor Walker.

In June 1912 an application was made to entirely rebuild the place, and the local magistrates were happy to grant this on condition that the new building included ladies' toilets. The applicant's solicitor said that 'the requirement of lavatory accommodation for women was in his experience an entirely novel one' and 'a burden he had never yet heard of being imposed on a licensed victualler'!

Extraordinarily this stumbling block resulted in the application being withdrawn. However, there seemed to have been a change of heart, and in October of that year rebuilding plans were approved.

The pub was given a major facelift in 1973 and in 1999 was renamed Doyle's bar, and became an Irish theme pub. This seemed rather unnecessary as the pub had long been a venue for Irish music and had many Irish customers. Happily the name was dropped in 2001 and the pub became the Grove again.

In 1905 the pub was at the centre of the activities commemorating the centenary of the death of Nelson. A large mast was erected outside the pub and at 8.00 am four buglers sounded the Reveille as the white ensign was raised to cheers from the crowd. Other flags and pennants used by Nelson were raised, and celebrations continued throughout the day and into the evening, including music from the police band, a 'cinematograph' display for the children at the Masonic hall and a high tea for the 'old folk' at Rutlish school. At 4.20 pm, the time of Nelson's death, the white ensign was lowered to half-mast and the Wimbledon Borough News reported that at that moment the sky blackened and a few drops of rain fell, only to go back to clear skies when the ensign was raised again. It will be interesting to see what commemorative activities take place in 2005.

Today the pub is owned by Punch Taverns.

MERTON ALE STORES 1953

HORSE & GROOM

This was formerly known as the Bricklayers' Arms (see separate entry) until 1882 when it acquired this new name under landlord James Cobb. In 1890 it still only had a beer and cider licence and was owned by John Oakman who also owned the Brewery Tap in Wimbledon Village, as well as other property locally. At this time the licensee was John Costin.

It was to retain this name for a hundred years until it was renamed the Dark House in 1984. For some reason the name changed back to the Horse & Groom briefly for a period between 1995 and 1996, but was changed again in 1997 to the Kilkenny Tavern (see below).

KILKENNY TAVERN

The current name of the pub at 131 Merton High Street formerly known as the Dark House, Horse and Groom, and Bricklayers' Arms. Today it consists of one large bar and is popular with cast members of TV's The Bill, Family Affairs, and various Irish actors. One commented that it was an 'easy pub to walk into, but difficult to walk out of'. He is said to have stayed a week on first visiting the pub!

MERTON PUB CRAWL

In 1999 CAMRA (Campaign For Real Ale) published Fifty Great Pub Crawls by Barrie Pepper. This book covered the entire country from Aberdeen to Arundel, and from Bury St Edmunds to Bath, so the author necessarily had to be very selective in his choice of areas to include. So it was a great honour for Merton to be included in this select fifty. The Merton pub crawl includes the Grove Tavern, Princess of Wales, Trafalgar, Princess Royal, Nelson Arms, William Morris, and Kilkenny Tavern. The Sultan and the King's Head are also included, which although in the borough of Merton, are not included in this book as they are in Wimbledon. The blurb on the back of Barrie Pepper's book assures us that all the crawls have been painstakingly tested by the grass roots experts of CAMRA to guarantee quality real ale. So high praise indeed for Merton's locals!

In addition to its many pubs, Merton also had plenty of off-licences. The one pictured opposite, in High Path, existed from around 1890 to 1953.

OLD LEATHER BOTTLE 1897

LEATHER BOTTLE

And this you may very well be sure
The Leather Bottel will longest endure
And I wish in Heaven his soul may dwell
That first devised the Leather Bottel
From a mediaeval drinking song

Along with the White Hart the Leather Bottle is one of the oldest of Merton's pubs. It is believed to date back to around 1700, but the first landlord recorded in lists of local victuallers is Edward Hubbart who was there in 1725. At that time the pub was in a different position to its present one at the junction of Kingston Road and Merton Hall Road. It was situated a little further to the east, roughly where the pub car park is now.

The fact that it was on the victuallers' list means that it was a properly licensed house, although judging by its size (the picture shows the original pub before the new one was built), a fairly modest one. It was closer to being a local tavern than a fully-fledged inn. It had a full spirit licence by 1890 and at that time was owned by Henry Walker and run by William Walker.

In 1897 an application was made for the new pub to be built in its present position (on the site of an old paddock) and the plan was to have a 'capacious' coffee room which could be entered without going through the bar. This, it was said, would be a great boon to cyclists and the 'large numbers' who used the nearby Polytechnic recreation ground. Despite this there were still objections from the Church of England Temperance Society who believed improved drinking facilities would be undesirable. The application however, was approved and the new building opened on May 26th the following year. The old building became a greengrocer's.

It is striking, despite the objections of temperance groups, how much pubs were used not just as drinking places, but as meeting places in the early part of the twentieth century. The Olde Leather Bottel Musical society was based there, as was the Slate club, and both groups held their annual dinners there. The Merton Park Cycling Club also met there.

Even in more recent years the pub has been the venue for jazz music in the 1970s (playing host to well-known names such as Humphrey Lyttleton, and George Chisholm), blues bands in the 1980s, and the alternative comedy Screaming Blue Murder club in the 1990s. Today it is still a venue for live bands. Another claim to fame for the pub is that the Rolling Stones' guitarist Ronnie Wood was a regular drinker here when he lived in Merton Park in the early 1990s.

Today the pub is owned by Scottish & Newcastle.

MERMAID

Souls of poets dead and gone
What Elysium have ye known
Happy field or mossy cavern
Choicer than the Mermaid Tavern?
John Keats 1795-1821

One of the most obscure of Merton's pubs, which was situated on the west side of Morden Road, close to where the Nag's Head stood until recently.

The Mermaid is mentioned in the census of 1841 but nowhere else. At the time it was simply described as the Mermaid beer shop and it was being run by one Samuel Hays who was described as a 'dealer'. So it looks as though, like the Anchor beer house round the corner in Kingston Road, the Mermaid was simply a sideline for a small businessman. Hays lived there with his wife and three children but what became of him we do not know.

It is possible that this beer shop was the predecessor to the Nag's Head which appeared in 1844, but as the locations of properties listed in the census were not precise it is impossible to be sure.

COFFEE TAVERNS

Between 1860 and 1880 the number of pubs in Merton almost doubled from eight to fifteen. Concerns about the evils of drink had been growing in this period and the first temperance meeting in Wimbledon was held in 1868.

By the following decade coffee houses and 'temperance inns' began appearing locally. The Bay Tree Temperance Hotel, which opened in 1878, was in the parish of Wimbledon, but standing as it did at the corner of Montague Road and Kingston Road would have served the people of Merton too.

By the 1880s, others nearby were the Hope Coffee Palace at 72 Merton High Street and the Single Gate Coffee House at Collier's Wood. There were several others in Wimbledon too.

Whether these had any direct effect on Merton's drinkers is hard to say, but by 1881 the Anchor beer house, almost opposite the Bay Tree in Kingston Road, had closed and by the following year the Plough at Merton Rush had gone too. It is likely though that these little beer shops, being sidelines for small businessmen, simply ended when the owners moved on or lost interest, and this may have been hastened by competition from other pubs rather than the coffee taverns. Perhaps the strongest argument for this is that all the other pubs had seen off the coffee houses and temperance taverns by the turn of the century.

NAG'S HEAD

If there's a heaven, which I do not doubt
There'll be an inn fire and a glass of stout
. If I can have just those two things
I'll do without my harp and wings
William Bernard 1947

John Denby was running this pub by 1844 when it was a simple beer house, just one of the many that sprang up in the wake of the 1830 Beer Act. The fact that this was just a mere three years after the 1841 census and that the Mermaid beer shop had already gone by then adds weight to the theory that this was a continuation of the same business.

One source suggests that after the death of Nelson large quantities of material from his mansion were used in the construction of the housing that was built on the 'Nelson's Fields' part of his estate and also in the building of this pub.

The pub was the venue for the annual village fair which was originally held at the White Hart in Kingston Road, but which was transferred from there when the railway came in 1855 and there was not enough space.

By 1890 the pub had a licence for beer, wine, and cider and was owned by the Attlee Brewery who also owned the Fox & Grapes and the King of Denmark in Wimbledon Village. At this time the licensee was one Thomas Scrogham.

The pub was rebuilt in 1937 and was here for another sixty years until it was demolished in 2001 to make way for flats. The pub had a paved garden at the back with a fishpond, and inside was what was known as the Sportsman's bar which had its walls adorned with pictures of sports stars.

As it was a free house rather than being owned by a brewery there is very little information available about its history.

NAG'S HEAD (JUST AFTER DEMOLITION 2001)

NELSON ARMS

So is it true that Lady Hamilton once lived here, that it is haunted, and that a secret tunnel runs underneath it?

This pub was started in 1829 by John Edney, who had previously served as a local constable. This was just six years after the last part of Lord Nelson's estate was sold off. The pub today is on the site of the entrance to the estate, so while it is close to where Lady Hamilton, and indeed Nelson himself, lived, it is not the same building. The present building only dates back to 1910; the original pub was slightly to the west along Merton High Street (see picture).

It was a properly licensed tavern rather than a simple beer house, opening as it did a year before the Beer Act had thrown open the role of beer retailer to almost anyone who could pay for the licence.

In the 1850s the Nelson Arms was run by Thomas Batt, formerly one of the Wimbledon Volunteers which had been formed in 1797 when it was thought that Napoleon may invade England.

By 1890 the pub was owned by brewers Day & Noakes, their only pub in Merton, and was being run by Alfred Fulman.

There was a tragedy here in 1900 when the landlord, Lewis Varney, died aged 52 as a result of alcoholism. It was said that the post-mortem recorded that his liver was twice the normal size.

But the pub itself was a pleasant place. The writer, Leopold Wagner, singled out the Nelson as the only pub in Merton to be mentioned in his book More London Inns and Taverns (1926).

He describes it as 'as enchanting a hostelry as anyone might wish to beguile his time in'. Wagner also records that it contains the 'nearest approximation to a smoke room in the provincial sense that a licensed victualler all London round can boast of'.

He writes that it has 'bowling green baize-top tables, armchairs, ferns and box plants, pictures and illustrated periodicals. Everything conducive to suggest a superior clubhouse'. He concludes: 'The Nelson Arms of Merton would repay a whole day's journey to revisit'.

Local resident Violette Wright remembers that in the 1920s when she was eight years old she was sent on a daily errand to the jug room which faced onto Abbey Road. Every day except Sunday she would take a china jug to the Nelson to collect half a pint of ale and half a pint of porter for an elderly lady neighbour. For this she was paid two pence a week.

She also remembers that in the bar sat an old man named Billy who had a tin bath full of watercress that he'd picked in Mitcham. He used to tie this in bunches with raffia and sell it for a penny a bunch to pay for his beer and bread and cheese.

NELSON ARMS 1898

There were also tales of a tunnel under the Nelson being used as an escape route when the local bobbies arrived to break up a gambling game. This is possible but to date no one has established the exact location of the tunnel. W.H. Chamberlain maintains that the tunnel ran across Merton High Street from number 39, which was a dozen buildings away from the Nelson Arms, while another source believes that the tunnel ran across the High Street from Lord Nelson's stables to the entrance lodge of the estate (where the Nelson pub was later built). The only certainty is that there was a tunnel running under what is now Merton High Street and that it was there before Nelson bought Merton Place in 1801.

There were also stories of a friendly ghost at the pub who was partial to the odd glass of port wine, but recent landlords have not reported any ghostly activity.

Today the pub retains the attractive tiled mural of a sea battle on its side wall and it is a link to the historic estate of Lord Nelson so sadly demolished over a century and a half ago.

Although the original name Nelson Arms remains on the wall of the pub, the sign reads: Nelson Bar. Today it is owned by Shannon Inns.

THE PLOUGH

This was a small beer house almost opposite the present Leather Bottle in Cross Row, at Merton Rush, a small group of cottages that once stood at the entrance of what is now Watery Lane. The pub was there by 1836 when it was known as Saunders' beer shop. By 1851 it was being run by William Jackson, and had been renamed the Plough.

The date of the Plough's closure is unclear but its proprietor, George Meek, had begun to be listed in local directories as 'builder' by 1874, and by 1882 had gone altogether. At that time the local grocer, Joseph Buddin had begun to sell beer, so perhaps the need for another beer house was no longer there.

This beer shop also played a small part in a local murder mystery of 1836 (see entry for White Hart).

PRINCE OF WALES c. 1920

PRINCE/PRINCESS OF WALES

When you have lost your inns drown your empty selves
for you will have lost the last of England
Hilaire Belloc

This pub, in Morden Road, first appeared in 1870, when it was being run by Thomas Cumby. By 1876 Young's (then Young & Bainbridge), had taken a lease on it. They bought the freehold in 1919 and still own it today.

In 1913 the Prince of Wales was mentioned by Hilaire Belloc in his book The Stane Street. Belloc was the first modern historian to make a detailed study of the old Roman road and he mentions that it passed very close to the site of the pub. This was later proved to be not precisely true but the line of the road was not far off. It is said that Belloc drank in the pub on more than one occasion while conducting his research.

The pub has also had some more recent well-known customers. The cast of TV's The Bill, who film in the area, are regulars, as are some of the cast of Channel 5's soap opera Family Affairs. Cast members of The Bill also joined in a protest to prevent the pub being closed in the mid-1990s. Young's had considered selling the pub and the site was to be used for a car showroom, but council planners refused permission.

In 1997, following the death of Diana, Princess of Wales, the pub was renamed in her honour by Young's after a suggestion by regulars. The pub's football team however decided to keep their original name, preferring not be known as the 'Princesses'!

The pub is also twinned with the Horse Brass pub in Oregon USA.

The pub retains a traditional atmosphere with none of the gimmicks that have spoilt some local pubs, and is almost an archetypal London local. It has a courtyard style garden at the back and the interior manages to be both spacious and homely.

YOU WILL ALWAYS BE MERRY AND
BRIGHT IF, WHEN IN TOWN, YOU VISIT

THE

'PRINCESS ROYAL'

ABBEY ROAD - MERTON

Good Beer, Good Food and
Good Service

Gardens open to the Public

Ladies and Children especially
catered for

∽∽∽∽∽∽∽∽∽∽∽

Proprietor - - **W. F. MOODY**

R.A.O.B. I.B.61 EVERY SAT. AT 7.30

PRINCESS ROYAL 1932

PRINCESS ROYAL

There is some mystery surrounding the beginnings of this pub in Abbey Road. According to documents in the possession of Courage, a former owner, the root of title goes back to 1850, when the freehold was sold for £860.00; the conveyance being between E. Howe and Charles Rowles. However, in the pub itself there is a copy of a lease dated May 31st 1859 between the owner, William Hodgson (of Hodgson's brewery) and Thomas Henden who leased the pub for £16.00 a year. So it is possible that the building was not a pub to begin with, but had become one by 1859. The first mention of Thomas Henden in local directories is in 1860.

By 1890 it was still owned by Hodgson & Sons Brewery and still only had a beer and cider licence. It was being run by a widow, Esther Lambert, who had taken over from previous licensee Peter Baker.

But the pub was known as the Princess Royal from the outset, and judging by pictures of it in the early and mid-20th century has changed little.

The corner door was closed off some time after Courage bought the pub in 1943, apparently because there had been accidents caused by passing traffic, and two of the bars have been knocked through into one, but apart from that it has remained a simple old-fashioned pub.

The Princess Royal is perhaps one of the best-kept secrets in Merton. A small, friendly local tucked away from the high street and possessing all the charm and atmosphere of a little country pub. It has a small courtyard style garden at the back and is a very cosy pub in the depths of winter.

It is also a favourite with CAMRA, the Campaign for Real Ale, whose South West London branch gave the pub an award for the longest run of Good Beer Guide entries - between 1983 and 1998.

The walls of the main bar are covered in pictures of film stars, and one of those pictured was a regular. Reggie Prince, who was a stunt double for Oliver Reed, drank at the pub until his recent death. Oliver Reed himself of course was a regular in many pubs in nearby Wimbledon.

Mercifully, the Princess Royal escaped the redevelopment that resulted in the High Path estate in the 1960s and is a haven for anyone who still enjoys a traditional pub free of gimmicks. Previously owned by Scottish & Newcastle it is now owned by the Unique Pub Company.

TRAFALGAR ARMS c.1900

TRAFALGAR ARMS

Merton's smallest pub, and the last remaining free house in Merton since the Nag's Head closed in 2001. The earliest mention of it in local records is in 1868 when proprietor William Prince is listed in the directory. The location is given as 'The Rookery' which was what the area between Morden Road, Merton High Street, and Abbey Road was sometimes known as. 'Rookery' seems to have been a generic term denoting poor, cramped housing.

In petty sessions records of 1890 it is shown that the pub was privately owned by Thomas Percival of Norman Road, Wimbledon, though it seems to have no connection with the Sultan pub in that road which was owned by the brewery Thorne Brothers. At that time the Trafalgar still only had a licence for beer and cider and was being run by one Robert Neal.

When the slum clearance took place in the 1950s to make way for the High Path estate the Trafalgar was spared. Perhaps it was thought it would be a focal point for the new development. One can still see the wall of the once-adjoining building in Pincott Road in place at the side of the pub.

Local resident Violette Wright remembers the pub being a 'rough place' in the early part of the twentieth century, used by some 'tough old men'. Also, it once had the nickname of the 'Threepenny Hop'. When the railway ran past the pub to the old Merton Abbey station, some men would get off the train and hop over the fence to the pub for a threepenny pint.

The single storey extension was built in 1906, and doubled the size of the pub, which is still small even now. The toilets were still outside, to the west of the pub, and after complaints from residents in the nearby cottages, inside toilets were eventually built in the 1930s.

Today it is a friendly street-corner local of the type that one may have thought would by now have vanished from London. Somehow it is always a surprise to find it there.

NELSON'S FIELDS

After Lord Nelson's estate was sold off in 1823 the area bounded by Morden Road, Merton High Street, Abbey Road, and High Path became known as Nelson's Fields. This was later covered in cheap housing for builders, labourers, mill staff and other low-paid workers. This perhaps explains why there were so many beer houses in and around the area in the Victorian era. Much of this cheap housing survived until the 1950s when the slum clearance programme was put into place, and part of what was Nelson's Fields was covered by the High Path estate.

NOTE: The picture opposite is believed to show the Trafalgar at the turn of the 20th century, though evidence for this is circumstantial and cannot be verified.

UNCLE TOM'S CABIN c.1920

UNCLE TOM'S CABIN

The predecessor to this pub, the Corner Pin (see separate entry) had been there since 1868, but in the 1890s the name was changed to Uncle Tom's Cabin. This little beer house, situated at the junction of Reform Place and Abbey Road, may already have been finding custom spread thinly between itself, the Nelson Arms and the Princess Royal, both within a hundred yards of it in Abbey Road, but in 1905 the licence itself was in jeopardy.

Local magistrates refused to renew it, partly on the grounds that other nearby pubs were more convenient. This decision was contested and at the ensuing meeting of the county licensing committee some interesting statistics were thrown up. Within a quarter of a mile radius of Uncle Tom's Cabin there were 958 houses, and serving their drinking needs were four fully licensed pubs, seven beer houses, and six off licences.

Uncle Tom's Cabin was described by the surveyor of the licensing magistrates as being originally two separate cottages, and as a 'dirty little cabin'. It was compared to the nearby Princess Royal and it was said that while the rooms at the Princess were not much bigger they were more airy and the pub stood on more ground. It was also noted that the two pubs catered for different types of clientele: the Princess Royal for passers-by, and Uncle Tom's Cabin for the 'poorer sorts of mechanics and artisans who stayed there until they were turned out'.

The licence was renewed, though a suggestion was made that the licence be transferred to another location within two years.

Two years on, in 1907, the magistrates refused to allow the owners, Phoenix Brewery, to rebuild the pub and so the licence, and the pub, ended. The building remained, and was converted into a corner shop, which was there until the 1950s redevelopment of the area.

In retrospect it is surprising that Uncle Tom's Cabin lasted as long as it did, being the third pub within a two hundred-yard stretch of a small side-street. But perhaps it illustrates how central pubs were to the social life of the community even as recently as the early 20th century.

NOTE: One can just make out the pub sign in the picture on the facing page. Although the picture was taken some years after the pub had ceased trading it is fortunate the sign had not been removed as this is the only known picture of Uncle Tom's Cabin.

WHITE HART c.1910

WHITE HART

Perhaps the most important of Merton's inns, and one of the two oldest. It was there by 1700, built on land which formed part of the bequest of William Rutlish.

In 1805 it was described as having 'cellars, stables, coach house, yard, and gardens', as well as 'three cow's commonings at the common within Merton'.

In 1823 the White Hart was the venue for the sale of Lord Nelson's estate. After Nelson's death in 1805 the house and estate had remained more or less as he had left them, but now the land was sold off in 'lots adequate for detached villas'. This was not how it turned out though. The area was to become known as Nelson's Fields and became a small community of poor housing served by several pubs and beer houses.

A lease of 1820 shows a cottage behind the inn consisting of a parlour, kitchen, and wash house – presumably for staff.

In 1845 the White Hart became a Young's pub! At least, it was leased from the trustees of the Rutlish charity by Young and Bainbridge until 1883, the yearly rent being £30.00 from 1862-1883. Young's do not appear to have made any attempt to buy the inn, and sadly it did not become one of their roster of excellent local pubs.

The White Hart gave its name to Hartfield Road. Just across the Kingston Road from the pub was the Hart Field and here the villagers would play games such as quoits and cricket. Sadly, the field was built over by 1870, but the name lives on to remind of us of what was once there.

The land at the side of the inn was the venue for the Merton village fair, but following the building of the railway line to Croydon in 1855 it was moved to the Nag's Head in Morden Road. W.H. Chamberlain recalls that a favourite event at this fair was the climbing of the greasy pole, with the prize of a leg of mutton for anyone who could climb to the top and retrieve a flag.

The pub itself remained largely unchanged apart from having a bottle and jug extension built in 1894 at the station side of the building, until it was bombed in the second world war.

In 1935 there was a double tragedy here when the landlord committed suicide in June, and then a barman committed suicide in November.

On June 20th about an hour after afternoon closing a potman heard gunshots from the bowling green at the rear of the pub. The Landlord, Edward Macey, was found with severe head wounds and an automatic pistol by his side. At the inquest it was said that he had been depressed due to gout and failing eyesight. He was 57.

Just five months later, on the 24th of November, barman David Robbins was found hanging by a rope in the cellar. Colleagues and family of the 37 year old could think of no reason why he would want to kill himself and the coroner recorded a verdict of suicide while of unsound mind.

Some years later it was said that following the two suicides the pub became known locally as the Rope & Gun.

After the pub was bombed during the war an application was made in 1945 to rebuild it, but this did not happen until 1958. Pictures of the pub in the 1950s show part of the roof missing.

The pub was refurbished in 1992, but in 1996 it was converted to an Irish theme pub and rechristened with the peculiar name of Bodhran Barney's (see Pub Names section). Thankfully, this was dropped and the pub became the White Hart again in 2001. Although the interior has changed radically from even a decade ago to an open-plan modern bar rather than a traditional pub at least it has kept the name with which so much local history is associated. It is now owned by the Contemporary Bar Company.

MURDER MYSTERY AT THE WHITE HART

As if the suicides, bombing, and other events were not enough to keep the White Hart in grim tales, there was also a murder mystery connected with the inn.

At 1.00 am on Sunday 17th of April 1836, Sarah and William Steel were awoken in bed in Watery Lane by voices arguing, and then a woman's scream. William Steele and another local resident, George Green, pulled the body of Harriet Haggerstone from the well in the street and took it to the White Hart.

She had been beaten up and drowned in the well. They then went to see her husband, David at their home, Mud Cottage (in what is now Cannon Hill Lane), and when he was told the news he wept. At 5.00 am the parish constable and the deputy overseer went to take David Haggerstone into custody, and he was released four days later. But why was he a suspect?

On the night before the murder Harriet had been drinking at the White Hart with railway worker William Claridge. Also there were William and Elizabeth Hedges, the Haggerstones' landlord and his wife. Harriet and Claridge left at 11.30 pm, and the Hedges went to Saunders' beer shop at Merton Rush. They left at 12.30 am, went home, and found David Haggertsone on the bed fully dressed. They asked him if his wife was home and he replied that he thought she was with them. They suggested that he should go back for her, but he refused, retorting 'I suppose she's at some of her whoring tricks'.

When told that she was dead, Haggerstone said 'Oh Claridge, you've done for me, why didn't you stop me?'

A night watchman had seen Harriet, Claridge and the Hedges outside the White Hart, and then go towards the Rush, but Elizabeth Hedges denied Claridge was with them.

Claridge said he and Harriet had walked to the beer shop and Haggerstone had arrived saying 'Damn your eyes woman, if you don't go home I'll murder you!' He said that Harriet and Haggerstone went home at 1.15 am while he went to find a bed for the night at the beer shop.

Claridge had also been arrested the same day as Haggerstone, and released after fourteen days. Haggerstone was then rearrested and sent for trial. He was charged with the wilful murder of his wife either by 'striking her divers mortal blows on her head, face, and other parts of her body, or by thrusting her down by force and against her will into a certain well, and choking and suffocating her therein'.

But no one was convicted due to a lack of evidence. Justice Park criticised the practice of paying railway workers late on Saturday nights at beer shops and pubs which 'encourages dissipation and crime among the lower classes'.

So the mystery of who killed Harriet Haggerstone was never solved, and another strange tale was attached to the White Hart.

WILLIAM MORRIS 2002

WILLIAM MORRIS

St George he was for England
And before he killed the dragon
He drank a pint of English ale
Out of an English flagon
G. K. Chesterton 1874-1936

Although a modern pub it has some history, being housed as it is in one of the buildings that was part of the Liberty print works.

This building was the block shop, built around 1925 and used to store the wooden printing blocks that were used to pattern the textiles. It is believed to have replaced an earlier, wooden building.

The pub was opened in 1990 soon after the opening of Merton Abbey Mills market and is a popular place on the banks of the Wandle.

One modern claim to fame is that the pub has become a favourite with the cast and crew of TV's The Bill programme, who film nearby.

The pub is now owned by Broken Foot Inns.

ROYAL SIX BELLS c.1820

ON THE BORDERS

As mentioned in the introduction, several pubs one may have thought were in Merton are actually just outside the parish boundaries and have not been included in this book. One or two properly belong in a book on Wimbledon pubs, and others are too recent to have gained any significance, but the Royal Six Bells in Colliers Wood High Street has served the people of Merton for almost three centuries and played a part in its history. It has therefore been included here for its importance to Merton.

It dates back to at least 1750 when victualler Richard Hollamby had the original, weather-boarded inn built. It is possible that there was an earlier building on this site, but there is no record of it.

A lease of 1797 shows that it was a substantial inn having stables, outhouse buildings, yards at the back, gardens, two tenements and a coachmaker's shop. The lease also shows that the inn owned land and property opposite the Six Bells, comprising houses, outhouses, yards, gardens, orchards, watercourses, etc.

In the mid-19th century the inn was a meeting place for carriers who exchanged loads and bought or sold goods and livestock.

The pub was also the centre of attention on Derby day when the Prince of Wales, later Edward VII, used to stop here on his way to Epsom. Local resident James B. Bass described how, in the early years of the 20th century, the Six Bells yard would be crowded with people stopping for drinks while representatives of Thorley's Food gave out free samples to the horses. He also describes the excitement of the day and the throngs of people lining Merton High Street to see the crowds on their way to the races.

In 1925 W.H. Chamberlain recalled the 'crowds of people and every kind of vehicle along Merton High Street and Morden Road with refreshments, booths, stalls, and acrobats etc. making a Londoner's holiday'.

The pub is owned today by the Punch Pub Company and has just reopened (on July 25th 2003) under the new name of Riverside as a restaurant/bar. It has been completely refurbished and extended, though some original features have been kept, and the car park has been converted to a beer garden. It is also a venue for live jazz and blues music.

NOTE: The 1750 building was captured in a watercolour painting (reproduced here) completed in the early 1800s before it was rebuilt around the middle of that century. One source claims that the picture was painted by John Chessell Buckler (1793-1894), but this claim has not been substantiated. Buckler did paint several pictures of Merton College, Oxford, and perhaps it is this connection which has led to the assumption that he painted the picture of the Royal Six Bells, curiously named the Five Bells on the painting.

THE PUB NAMES

The names of pubs can be important as they often tell you something of the pub's history and local associations. The White Hart, for example, gives its name to Hartfield Road, and that association was lost when the pub temporarily changed its name. The William Morris reminds us of the fact that the famous craftsman had his premises nearby

Other pub names are more enigmatic. The Dark House, for example, has long been a mystery, even to most locals.

Not surprisingly there are several pub names connected directly with Lord Nelson: The Nelson Arms, The Trafalgar, the Victory (in Colliers Wood), and the Emma Hamilton. There are also others with seafaring themes/connections such as the Mermaid and the Anchor, and one, which although not believed to be named after a ship nevertheless has a sign showing one (the Princess Royal). Though whether any of these were so named because of Nelson it is impossible to say. It would be difficult to find any other explanation for so many sea-related names in any area so far from the coast.

Also, although there are not a great number of pubs in Merton there are some which have, or have had, unique names, such as the Emma Hamilton, and the Dark House.

A NOTE ON PUB SIGNS

Pub signs were in existence before pub names, and many names were derived directly from the signs. For example, a pub may have shown a picture of a leather bottle outside to denote that it was a drinking house, and in time people would refer to the 'house at the sign of the leather bottle'. Later, the pub would simply be known as the Leather Bottle and eventually this became the name.

However, in more recent times the sign makers and designers have often used some artistic licence to depict their interpretation of a pub's name. So we have local anomalies such as the Princess Royal, which although almost certainly named after one of Queen Victoria's daughters, nevertheless has a sign depicting a ship.

So a note of caution in reading too much into the picture on a pub sign – the name is more likely to give clues about its history.

ANCHOR

Not an uncommon name near a port or harbour, but why here, fifty miles from the coast? Anchor, it seems, does not just have a nautical meaning, but a religious one too, i.e. the stabilising effect of faith. It is thought to come from the words of St. Paul: 'Which hope we have as an anchor of the soul, both sure and steadfast and which entereth into that within the veil'. This particular beer house began in the era of the temperance movement, which was led by the church, so perhaps a name with religious overtones may have been thought to add some respectability to the enterprise.

BEEHIVE

The beehive is seen as a symbol of industry, and the location of this beer house in Nelson's Fields puts it at the heart of a small community of working-class people who worked in the nearby factories and mills. The Nelson's Fields area was densely populated and was no doubt as busy as the proverbial beehive.

BODHRAN BARNEY'S

The name given to the White Hart in the 1990s aroused some controversy and not a little bewilderment – what on earth could it mean? Bodhran, pronounced 'Bawran' is an Irish tambourine, so it simply seems to have been chosen to convey the fact that the pub had become an Irish theme pub. The pub's emblem showed an Irish dancer holding a bodhran.

BRICKLAYERS' ARMS

Pubs named after trades were common in areas where the pubs wished to attract local working-class artisans. From 1830 there were many new beer houses competing with the longer established inns and taverns and it made sense for them to aim straight at the clientele for whom they were catering. Niche-marketing as it would be called today.

CORNER PIN

A pun essentially. The corner pin is the outside skittle in the old pub game of Nine Pins, but in this case it simply refers to the fact that the pub was on a corner.

DARK HOUSE

The Horse and Groom in Merton High Street was nicknamed the Dark House for many years and in 1984 was officially renamed with this odd moniker. There seems to be no other pub in the country with this name, and no one seems entirely sure how it came about. The pub sign gives no clue, showing, as it does, two gentlemen in period clothing sharing a drink. Oddly, the sign does not seem to relate directly to the pub's previous names, the Horse and Groom, or the Bricklayers' Arms, either.

One explanation for the name Dark House is that it was one of the last pubs in the area to have electricity, and the relatively dim gas lighting gave rise to its nickname. Some have suggested the pub was the scene of dark deeds. Others have put forward the simple theory that due to its position the pub gets little sunlight. Whatever the real reason, one drinker points out that although the pub has undergone several name changes, it will always be known locally as the Dark House.

DOG & PARTRIDGE

A hunting reference of course, but why here? There is no record of game hunting in the area so perhaps it was simply that the first landlord was keen on the sport.

DUKE OF CAMBRIDGE

George, Duke of Cambridge was an important local land owner in the Victorian era, owning much of the Coombe area which was later cut through by the Kingston by-pass which runs past the door of this pub.

Until 2001 there was also another Duke of Cambridge pub at the side of the Kingston by-pass near the Robin Hood gate of Richmond Park.

EARL BEATTY

Born in 1871, David Beatty was the first Earl Beatty and became Admiral of the Fleet and Earl in 1919 after distinguished service in the First World War. During the war he had served with Earl Jellicoe (see below). Prior to this he had been naval secretary to Winston Churchill and the youngest flag officer for a century. He died in 1936 and two years later this new pub was named after him.

EARL JELLICOE

The first name suggested for what was eventually to become the Emma Hamilton – but who was Earl Jellicoe? The short answer is another English admiral. Perhaps it was felt Nelson already had enough pubs in Merton named after him and his associations

He was born in 1859 and at the beginning of the First World War was appointed Commander-in-Chief of the Grand Fleet. He became First Sea Lord in 1916 and Admiral of the Fleet in 1919. He was made an Earl in 1925 and died in 1935. He would therefore have been in the minds of the people who were looking for a name for the pub in 1936.

EMMA HAMILTON

One of the few local pubs whose name has a cast-iron provenance. As mentioned previously, it was chosen by the public and is of course named after Lord Nelson's celebrated paramour. The only pub in the country with this name.

GROVE TAVERN

Named after the large house which once stood near the north west corner of Kingston Road and Merton Road and known as Merton Grove. It had been built in 1792 by Sir Richard Hotham who had also built Merton Place, later the home of Lord Nelson.

HORSE & GROOM

One of the more common pub names, which in this particular case, being a new name for the Bricklayers' Arms, seems to have been an attempt to go 'upmarket'. There may also be an element of punning in this name as the landlord who changed it to this was named Cobb – 'cob' being a small horse.

KILKENNY TAVERN

The current name of the preceding pub. Named in 1997 after the home town of the leaseholder.

LEATHER BOTTLE

Simply the name of an old-fashioned drinking vessel. It was also the symbol of the Bottlemakers' Company and the Horners' Company. In its local context it conjures up images of farm workers taking beer with them to drink as they worked in the fields of nearby farms such as Merton Hall Farm.

MERMAID

Another of the strangely inappropriate nautical references locally. The only explanation may be that in the hero-worship following the death of Nelson nautical references became popular. Again, there may be a pun at work here with the 'mer' of Merton transposing to the pub name.

NAG'S HEAD

According to Lesley Dunkling and Gordon Wright early versions of this sign sometimes indicated that horses could be hired from the inn, but this pub was originally a simple beer house and was unlikely to have had stables adjoining. So it seems there was no specific reason for this name here.

NELSON ARMS

There are reputed to be more pubs named after Nelson than after any other individual. Though here at least there is a sound local connection with the celebrated admiral. The pub was built close to the site of the entrance to Nelson's estate and within twenty-four years of his death. Very few of the many other pubs named after Nelson can claim to have such a genuinely direct connection with him.

PLOUGH

Another common name, and clearly one that was designed to appeal directly to local farm workers. This beer house at Merton Rush would have been handy for workers at nearby Manor Farm, Merton Hall Farm and Bakers End Farm as well, perhaps, as other local farms further afield.

PRINCE OF WALES

This name almost certainly refers to Prince Edward, later Edward VII, who was the eldest son of Queen Victoria, and lived from 1841-1910.

PRINCESS OF WALES

The above pub underwent a name change following the death of Diana, Princess of Wales, in 1997. Although there were other pubs with this name, this one appears to be the first one in the country to have been renamed after Diana.

PRINCESS ROYAL

Princess Royal is the title given to the first daughter of the reigning monarch, and this pub was probably named after the first daughter of Queen Victoria, also named Victoria. The present pub sign however, shows a ship (yet another nautical connection) which may have mistakenly have been believed to be one of Nelson's ships. Nelson did sail in a fleet containing a ship named Princess Royal in 1795, but he was captain of another ship, the Agamemnon.

ROYAL SIX BELLS

The pub was originally known simply as the Six Bells, and the name is believed to derive from the use of bells by wagoners to signal their approach. At the time this inn was built in the mid-eighteenth century the leading horse of the train of horses and wagons approaching the inn would sound its own distinctive bells. The 'Royal' was added much later when the Prince of Wales, later King Edward VII, used to regularly stop here to change horses en route to the Epsom races.

SHIP

One mystery that has long confounded local historians is the entry in the 1832 directory listing 'The Ship' at Merton under its inns. There is no other mention of an inn of this name in censuses, maps, or other documents, but it seems to be simply a case of mistaken identity, or perhaps even laziness on the part of the directory compiler.

Just outside the parish of Merton in Colliers Wood High Street was the Victory, which of course, was named after Lord Nelson's famous ship. The inn sign would probably have depicted the vessel, and this was duly noted down by the representative of the directory as The Ship.

TRAFALGAR ARMS

This is another Nelson reference of course, this time commemorating the location of his last battle and demise. The pub is also situated within the area that was once part of Lord Nelson's estate, later known as Nelson's Fields, and as such has a direct connection with the ubiquitous admiral.

UNCLE TOM'S CABIN

The word 'cabin' again has nautical connotations, but the name comes of course from the book Uncle Tom's Cabin by Harriet Beecher Stowe. Published in 1852, the story of a black slave found resonance with many of those who supported not only the emancipation of slaves, but also of women, and the working class in general.

This little beer house, catering for the more humble of Merton's residents, perhaps benefited from this association.

WHITE HART

This was the heraldic symbol of Richard II, but because of its popularity as an inn sign came to be almost a generic name for an inn. So although its name had no local significance the pub gave its name to the field opposite and in turn to Hartfield Road. An instance of the local place deriving its name from the inn rather than vice versa.

WILLIAM MORRIS

Perhaps this pub should have been called the Arthur Liberty. After all it is housed in one of the old block shops of his print works. William Morris's premises were situated where the Savacentre stands today. But the reputation of the celebrated craftsman, poet, and socialist undoubtedly looms larger than that of Arthur Liberty both in Merton and elsewhere, and in any event Liberty refused use of their name at the site after they left so the William Morris it became.

ACKNOWLEDGEMENTS

Ruth Murphy
Special thanks to Violette Wright for invaluable personal reminiscences
Merton Local Studies Centre
Wandsworth Local Studies Centre
Surrey History Centre
Tom Kean and regulars at Trafalgar Arms
Paul Dixon and regulars at Princess Royal
Matthew Woodville (Youngs brewery)
Peter Hopkins
Eric Montague
Special thanks to David Roe for providing information on pub names and signs and for helpful suggestions with the typescript
Special thanks to Judy Goodman for providing valuable source material, offering helpful suggestions with the typescript, and answering many queries

PHOTOGRAPHS

Dark House – Wandle Industrial Museum
Dog & Partridge – Merton Library Service
Duke of Cambridge – Keith Every
Merton Ale Stores – Merton Library Service
Old Leather Bottle – Merton Library Service
Nelson – John Innes Society
Prince of Wales – Young's brewery
Princess Royal – Courage
Royal Six Bells – Merton Library Service
Trafalgar (1953) – Merton Library Service
Trafalgar (1900) – Keith Every
Uncle Tom's Cabin – Merton Library Service
White Hart (p. 38) – Keith Every
White Hart (Front cover) – Wimbledon Society Museum
All others – Author's own collection

BIBLIOGRAPHY

Reminiscences of Old Merton – W. H. Chamberlain
Inn and Around London – Helen Osborn
John Innes and the Birth of Merton Park – John Innes Society
Pictorial History of Merton and Morden – Judith Goodman
Kingston Then and Now – Margaret Bellars
Merton Park the Quiet Suburb – John Innes Society
Once Upon a Time - James B. Bass
History and Heroes of Merton – Kathleen Denbigh
Dictionary of Pub Names – Lesley Dunkling and Gordon Wright